North River Songs

Charlie Brannick

North River Songs

Dedicated to

Mother and father who always wanted me to write home more often. To my wife's parents for their gift of my wife whose love and trust I treasure. For my nephew Chris, talented and funny, who left us too soon. For those I loved, and friends who went different ways.

Table of Contents

Beginnings

Aℓℓ summer long while the tomatoes ripened on the vines and the leafy rhubarb grew, mom with grandma's help looked after the two little girls. At dinner, the setting sun would shine through the back window across the small kitchen table getting into dad's eyes and he would have to get up and pull the shade. After dinner, they'd eat the sweetened rhubarb and drink iced tea and talk about the coming baby, "as long as you and the baby are ok" he'd say, himself practically an orphan, his mom dying when he was three and being raised by and aunt and uncle. For his birthday, maybe he'd get a pear and for Christmas a pair of socks and some new shoelaces.

All summer long mom grew like a tomato in the hot humid Jersey summer before air conditioning. The Yankees led by Phil Rizzuto and Joe DiMaggio were in a pennant race with the Red Sox and the Indians. The Red Sox had Ted Williams and the Indians the flame thrower Bob Feller. By October with the scent of burning leaves in the gutters and the sound of the crowd and marching band coming

from the high school football field on the hill, and Red Barber's

voice coming from the tv in the living room in the first ever televised

World Series, when for the first time in a decade a New York team

would not be in it, between the Cleveland Indians and the Boston

Braves, I came into this world and would be their first son. I would

bear his name as his father did and walk these Valley streets as he

and his father did before me.

The rest of the Valley would go on about their business under

beautiful October skies and the few who took note were happy for

them. In this life where there are so few meaningful relationships

and where we are basically on our own, as long as I could find

somebody to love, and who would love me in return, I knew I would

be ok.

When I would ask

for a good baseball glove or fishing gear I was given something

but not what I wanted. You don't know how good you have it

I was told.

In our house we bought groceries, gas, heat, clothes,

the house and used car had to be paid for,

they saved for a family vacation,

the church got a little and they put some away

just in case.

When you get your own money, you can buy whatever you want.

"You don't know what you want", he'd say.

So, get busy, don't waste your time in school.

That's how you get a better job.

If not school then work, nobody gives you anything in life.

And when you do buy something, buy something that will last.

Don't just throw it away on junk.

My mother said that.

And there it was.

The blueprint for my life.

I remember

the day the final cuts were made

sitting in the bleachers when uniforms were being given out.

One of the older guys Nicky

asked the coach if any of us

were good enough for the majors?

And Tony said flatly," nah, maybe Ontario "

killing any hope. My heart dropped

like a rock and I thought

what is this guy talking about?

Can't he see we made this team?

And what a great team it is?

This can't be the final word

I'm only ten years old.

And by God Ontario did make a run

at the majors, 8 years in and out

with the Cardinals.

World Series Champs

Tony sat us down

and read us the lineup

Chris Kreeck would be in Left

with a rocket arm and a flop of brown hair

his older brother Geoff

had blonde hair and the look of a Viking.

Their dad drove a van

with their name and electrical contractor

on the side.

Matt Maruky was in Center

where he'd roam like a mustang

and laugh like a hyena

when he'd scare you with one of his wild pitches.

The cement that held the team together

was Buddha at Short and Ontario at 3rd.

And both would pitch.

Tony said: "chatter"

and it was like Buddha's native tongue.

I was the weak link at 2nd for sure.

Blues was a big target at 1st

and gravel faced Nicky who looked like a Turk

was behind the plate.

Hambone a light skinned negro was in Right

and the Looch, Ronnie G. and G. G. Hambone's little brother

were backups.

We won every game and were home by noon

to tell mom about it at lunch

then back over the park for more.

In 8th Grade

Miss Domazewski asked,

"what we wanted to be when we grew up?"

And I said a professional baseball player.

She said "that was foolish

and only a very, very few could do that."

But what did I care what she said? It was my life.

What I really liked was sports.

What yacking year was that anyway 1962?

When the Cowboys broke their 99-game losing streak

and beat Freehold High 13-6.

When Richie Catalbo found Joe Tanner

on the other end of a 24-yard wounded duck

of a pass in the end zone that got the job done

and bedlam ensued.

The crowd swarmed the field and by God they went right

for the wooden goal posts and they rocked and rocked and

creaked until they cracked and came down. I thought

I was at West Point witnessing some grand tradition.

Them Cowboy fans knew how to get a party started.

I was ecstatic and walked home on clouds and delivered

the family the news on trombone and cymbal.

Hanging out with my friends.

(Le Jardon formerly known as The Store or Timmy's)

The Store

Mid 60's it was and the music was hot

4 Seasons were the favs, Beach Boys, Tempts and 4 Tops

A time in their lives when a dad's work is done

the hangout on the corner was claiming their sons

A leaderless group with nothing to do

some Irish, Italian a couple were Jews

on a good night, there they were some 40 strong

talking and laughing and carrying on

Outside, inside, outside again

struttin' and puffin' all amongst friends

spill over the sidewalk leaning on cars

boys to men from Valley Road that's who they are

Timmy was fun and an unpredictable cat

short like a jockey t-shirt and sandals no hat

His Candy Store, juke box, counter and grill

smokes, cokes and pinball all paid the bills

Timmy needed us like we needed him

a place in this world where he could fit in

He was the star and The Store was his stage

the cast of characters would fill up a page

Nicknames that kill like Buddha, Blues and Danny Magoo

Cheet, Boff, Mugs and Beanpole too

All of them hanging with nothing to do

Just hanging, idling and being a pain

driving the tax paying neighbors insane

before the cops lock us up we better go for a cruise

hop in a car turn up the rhythm and blues

I call shotgun the rest pile in

working' the radio past the other end

Up to the Pancake house where we'll beat the check

see if we can make in down Eagle Rock

with no hands and no wreck

Back to the Store now this night's on the ropes

we gave it our best but at this point no hope

no one wants to go home as tight as we are

listen to the radio a little more in the car

Then with a yawn comes the first hint

they're cashing it in now it's just you

on the sidewalk by the streetlight at this hour alone?

With my friends all gone I guess it's time to go home.

I liked the old days

when Elmer had the Pool Hall

and Jimmy Chan delivered mail

for every Butch with an Impala

there were ten who lusted after this Holy Grail

Buddy walked home with Sally

every day from school

the rest of us went cruising

thought shotgun was pretty cool

you had your friends

and how that made you feel

One by one they get distracted

locked up or lost in traffic

the herd begins to thin

you're left twisting in the wind

for every Spring that blossoms

there's a Fall that brings an end

a long time between loves

and times without a friend

We probably have the hardest jobs

to leave the boys to act like men

God give us strength

to face our days

upright in every way

and someone who is there for us

to share with us

at the end of every day.

The Cops

would usually still be moving when they would roll down the window and shout "keep moving" as they made their rounds. Heads down in mock repentance we'd head east and west and return in 5 minutes. We were the baby boomers on the bend in Valley Rd.

Sometimes they'd grab one or two and make you sweat. " Get in the car". Would they call our parents? Would it go on our record? Maybe take us to the station and then release. One day under pressure from the tax paying neighbors they came from every direction and rounded up 17 of us. This time it was for real and we would have our day in court.

They had a Court in City Hall and real serious Italian judge. He laid out the charges and the possible consequences and we gave our excuses. My Dad was there, he must have been on vacation at the time and from the back row he muttered " all bums". To which I was

so embarrassed and thought my friends would kill me with ridicule

but we were sent home and nobody said anything and nothing

changed.

Only Time could get us off that bend in the road. College courses,

the Vietnam War, a serious relationship, things like that had the

power to move us from the sidewalk in front of Harry's, Timmy's

Confectionary, Sal the Barbers', Kingsley Liquors or the Egg Store.

And nowadays you'll find most of the cast scattered across the

middle class of America. Except maybe Mark Margnanty who I

heard owns a deluxe hamburger shop in Thailand.

Back to The World

One week after I was back in "the world "I would turn 21 and the

Mets would win their first World Series. A few months later in the

Spring the Knicks would win their first NBA title. The first night

home I went down to the corner in a careful manner and there was

Marco who I had known from before and now he was one of the few

remaining survivors. He was caught up in Mets fandom and I was

right at home with that so for me this was an easy way to strengthen

our bond. My wartime experience would run counter to the current

scenario so it was best to keep it under wraps.

I thought I earned some free time. Like a complete life's worth. I

thought being back in the "world" and being "free" would be an exciting feeling that would carry me forward but that feeling doesn't last and the euphoric sense of freedom dissipates one empty weekend at a time.

People either changed or stayed the same. If you changed and caught on you got a new life and another chance. I started hanging with Marco and Todd. Marco was a social bug and Todd was a freak but freaks were in and they both seemed to know a lot of people. I could start by letting my hair grow. About halfway to freakdom like Mick Jagger's might do since I still might have to dance with the straight world. Maybe then I could serve both masters?

That Spring I took a job as a landscaper and my skin tanned and my muscles tightened as my hair grew to a proper length. I got a job evenings parking cars at Rod's Roadhouse as I was falling back into my old ways of working and saving. The music and the styles were changing. The girls I went to school with were finishing college and out of circulation. At nightclubs, we just stood along the walls and tried to make conversation over loud music. One night Marco came up where I was working and said "c'mon" meaning what are you doing here? In a way, he was right. In a way, he was wrong. I got in the car and started off in a new direction.

We did a lot of cruising. Marco usually knew where he was going. Marco was bringing me up to speed on the music as he drove. One day he saw someone walking by herself and said, "there's Tasha" pulling over like the car was on fire. She was moving along with a happy rhythm and pace. When he called she leaned in like a flower bends from the stem and came our way like the fragrance on the wind. On the Camaro window her face was a lighted butterfly, her eyes and smile fluttering wings. She played along like a kitten with a string. Marco threw introductions in the air like flower petals. One for her. Another for me... And then a couple more we made when our eyes met and we said "Hi".

She was a precocious flower that you had to have eyes to see and a guide to show you. It felt good to get introduced to somebody even if she was young. She was somebody and now so was I. It takes a little thing like that to get it going. To get yourself going. I was in the stream of life now that flowed from street corner, to the streets, to the flowers in secret gardens. She buzzed and flitted around from flower to flower and garden to garden. She seemed like a free agent exploring the world. A world that was changing and now hope seeds with our names on them were scattered to the ground. Like an investor with a handful of stock the future held promise. I was supposed to be well on my way through college but instead I was free and going for a ride. I thought no more of it as we rolled along, the world opening up before us like a garden in spring ready to pop.

We'd ride around in Marco's car and he'd play the music. We'd practice fake dialogues in hippie tones to see if we were getting it right, mocking others as we did. Soon I was caught up in a fever to be in the right places. My parents gave me the downstairs unit which was a powerful move on their part. I had my stereo which I bought with money I saved in Vietnam. Marco would play DJ and for a tune he wanted us to get he'd say "listen, listen" and then turn it way up shaking his head with his hair flying in all directions for emphasis. We smoked our weed and drank some booze as the de facto way of steeling our courage. Marco usually had a sense of where we should go. He'd say "I'm bored" which was a cue. Then we'd go somewhere like Don's, or the park in St. Cloud looking for people.

It was the scene we were looking for. No invitation was necessary just put yourself in it. Don't try to take over just be part of it. Go by feelings and try to read minds. Read and be read and see what happens.

People talk in new phrases that go nowhere. Our plain lives were competing with Rock Stars. They're saying things that aren't meant to go anywhere just sprinkle the earth with the sound of their voices.

They say things like lyrics to a song that don't demand your attention, they seek it and if not fall harmless to the ground like light rain. If I was sure of myself I might sprinkle the earth with some of my own but I'm more like a cloud and nobody knows what's inside.

Nobody knows where this is going but there are restless impatient feelings of youth at work under these cool exteriors. We're all in the same boat looking for something. A bold move could be uncomfortable like direct sun or a strong wind. My head was a TV show where no one dared touch the channel. Some people have cameo roles but those I don't take serious. It's the stars I follow that have put something in me.

My hope is that the right one will pick up the feeling like a soft breeze across calm water. There'll be an island we can drift to. The first one to see it or feel it can holler. If your excitement is genuine points could be scored and would be as welcome as a trade wind on a hot day but a faked effort will fail. No points, no laughs, no inroads, no first down, no forgiveness for a bad call. Better to feel stifled and choked and save what confidence you have for the right moment. Just be there and hang. The earth holds all its pieces together in a delicate balance. Tread softly and wait as calm as you can for the coolness of dusk and the new light of the moon.

Everybody wants to bump up their status. Poke their heads above water by clothes, looks, by the way you speak, your silence, your knowledge, by what music you like, or whatever you have going for yourself at the same time afraid of looking and sounding different. Unless you have something better to do you hang. You put your personality in chains as you wait it out with a patience that kills.

Words are swords that cut or make inroads. Don't hurt anyone or upset the balance. Let the natural order flow and the young chicks strut. Of course they want you to be there. It's your flaws that make them stars. You're part of the show. It's just the words that are hard to find. The ones that put the right people together. When you left those words come tumbling out exactly as you want. Replaying countless scenarios always with you winding up with the right chick deeply in love and bound together by understanding.

I was a Viet Vet and not really embarrassed by my service. I'm not sure how this feeling will go over. Nobody asks for it so I don't tell. Nobody asks for anything from me. I just watch and read what's going on. I see one I like a lot. She says little things like "what sign are you?" or "I love this song", directed at nobody and I let it fall like light rain. She goes on about Jethro Tull and Aqua Lung and I'm amused by the names. She's the center of attention who has more leeway than others and a greater margin for error. I see no mistakes or fault in her being and if I did I would embrace it.

My mind searches for the keys to open doors. Where two people can be themselves and use the plain language that everyone knows and flows easily. Watching and waiting was killing me. It was a time when each flower was blooming. Each one beautiful and swaying towards one future or another. I had an unspoken fever sick crush on Jasmine and Tasha would flirt and annoy me at the same time strutting about in front of me tempting and teasing and drawing me out to look like a fool. Someone bolder than I might come along and pick them up and when they returned it could be different or totally ruined. I had to be there. Everybody I cared about was here. No place better to spill your blood. If you die it was on the inside and nobody would know.

The things you were sure of in this world didn't matter. It was something new that would have to be discovered that I searched for. What could I say that would feel good like warm sun or be refreshing as summer rain? Marcos' approach with his stuttering and hesitation, all fake and contrived worked best. He was still here and held better ground than I even if I could see no breakthrough for him either. Better to follow Marco's lead and wait here like a farmer with his elbow on his shovel. Everything I wanted to grow would come up right out of this field.

I'm not good with light stuff and to try might tire or bore them. Any lie I tell them might be sniffed out. All I can think of is my love is so strong it will be the best thing, better than the things they already know. I have a time convincing myself to say that.

By the next spring I took a job as a Sky Marshall and had to go away for a while. I was back before the start of summer and had a job which took me to the major cities of Europe. I was never gone long, usually just an overnight stay and part of the next day before I'd return.

When I returned it was always with the same hunger for what I may have missed. For who was gaining ground. For who had moved an inch. Still rushing away from the dinner table to be with friends. I was home from Vietnam almost two years now and didn't feel lost.

My heart was fully engaged in what I was doing. There was no place else I'd rather be.

I couldn't see straight for Jasmine the cute blonde and Tasha flirting from a distance and up close at the same time. I didn't know where I stood only that I was in the midst of a beautiful garden. Why did I let my feelings go like this with high school girls I don't know? There are rules like society's and rules like biology's and chemistry's that set your heart pounding. There's ones the guys on the street corner have that say you don't take young chicks like this serious but my dad was six years older than my mother how does that fit in with this? Then there's other rules about timing containing the painful lessons of history about hesitation and missed opportunities. New rules were changing the culture and shaking things up all around the world so who knew where this would wind up? Who is in charge and who sorts it all out and steers my body where it should go?

My old life was ambling through high school burning only for sports or at the mercy of Vietnam hoping to return, now here I was burning for this. Here it was on my home turf where I'm picking up wounds and dying playing along in a stupid game. Stupid game with stupid rules. Stupid life I'd have to figure out. I'm supposed to be free and living instead of picking up wounds and dying. Picking up purple hearts on the home field from friendly fire. Why can't I find a simple scenario with one girl and a green field before us?

One night at Don's while the others were inside Tasha and I were left alone. I felt something honest and unfiltered rise from within and I let it out and it struck her as funny. What came back from her sent the soda shooting through my nose. The choked-up emotions broke like a dam and the earthquake and the aftershocks kept coming shaking us with laughter. Todd was nearby and saw what was happening but he tipped the balance and self-awareness kicked in. No longer were we in the free flow zone racking up points. It was a good feeling though and a sign that we could get on the same

wavelength again.

We saw each other after that just enough to keep it alive but she was

17 and still had a year of high school to go. It was all over now for

me. I had made the transition back. I was found and little else

mattered. I was pretty much sick and couldn't think of anything else.

Breaking Away

Many roads

lead out of town

go ahead try

to make something of your self

stay true to the dream

neither too careful or too reckless

Time is a wild untamed river

that carries us all

but this is the good I find

where my thoughts, works and love all flow,

give thanks for the chance

and make the most of the gift.

I thought a JC in Boston would be a good place to get some space

and separation. It turned out to be one of my loneliest years. I felt

weird as a Vet among all these mommy and daddy's kids. I could

have just as easily flipped the script and used it to my advantage but

that wasn't me. I was struggling with feelings of being not good

enough. Probably because I was young and hadn't done anything yet but I didn't know this one thing then. That satisfaction and true self-worth come from doing things well and doing something you're proud of.

The rooming house I lived in was creepy as hell but all I could afford. I was the first Vet to apply for G.I. benefits at this college and I had to wait practically the whole year for the checks to come. With nothing else to do I got all A's. I read all the time. Anything too. Boston was like that. I remember an old guy with a scruffy beard in working man's clothes walking down the street with groceries in one arm and books in the other. It was like "a spirit of learning" hovered over the town.

Anything that was free I would do. If there was time to kill between classes I'd walk over to the Public Library or the Financial District. Sometimes all the way downtown to "the Combat Zone" and by the old Boston Garden. Free lectures, free plays, I devoured the free weekly newspaper the Phoenix and looked forward to each addition.

Free rallies at the Commons. I'd walk from the Commons to

Brookline. On nice days, I might detour at Kenmore Square and get

lost in a daydream looking out onto Fenway Park. Seeing the field

from the sidewalk home of the Red Sox. Other days with more time

I'd walk over the Charles River to Harvard Square. What a strange

place for our leaders to come from I thought. Walking and looking

were free and in that way, I saw Boston.

I budgeted enough for bus fare to be home for the holidays. I tried to

sneak in a few extra returns hitch hiking. One time I teamed up with

a good-looking co-ed I met at the freeway on ramp. She was going

somewhere in South Jersey. We got one ride that took us all the way.

When the guy dropped me off right in front of my house I felt a little

sad for her having to go the rest of the way alone. Or sad that we

were developing this bond now severed most likely forever. Other

guys might have tried to make a move. She wore decent clothes and

me in my shabby leather I got from a second-hand store. I could have said what's your # I don't have one? I'll call you. You want to walk around with me when we get back to Boston? We could visit anything that was free? We could go back to my room and listen to the radio? I lacked imagination or beset with inferiority feelings IDK? Whatever it was I let it pass, when you look back on it we had a lot in common. Same age, college in the same town, willing to hitchhike home. She might have had a similar spirit? Or maybe we would just be a mismatch and a distraction to what each of us was trying to do?

Other times taking the Trailways home riding over the Tapanzee Bridge entering the City from the north. It was winter time and it got dark early. So much foot traffic on the busy uptown street. Passing all the lit up bodegas with unique food items you'd never find in my neighborhood. I felt envious of all those people with lives and passions they could satisfy. The people knowing how to navigate around all the vagrants lurking in doorways and congregating on drug corners. Knowing where to go and what choices to make. Life in the big city as simple as that. Knowing where to go and what choices to make and in the end getting somewhere.

I lived in an atmosphere of reading and solitude. An intense struggle marked my existence. Not even sure what I was wrestling with. What was this hard edge that showed up on my face and kept others away? To me other college kids looked happy, innocent and free. One night as I was bottoming out I had this liberating thought. I had just proven something to myself.

I went to this town with a plan and very little else and survived. If I did this here I could do this anywhere. It was powerful and gave me a surge of confidence going forward. Spring was breaking out and I realized I had made it.

This hard edge of intensity

I live by

I struggle with it by daylight

if I fight back hard

it breaks

If I try to escape

it scrutinizes my every step

It marks my existence

an irritant to my peace

If I'm working

it slowly dissipates

softens its grip

and finally, there is peace

I am man

and what else can I do?

Ambition

Where the world don't care

it's your job to make it

leave as big a hole in it

as you can

let them try to fill it.

Every pup

thinks he's an Alpha

and something out there upsets me

I charge to the door barking

I need to get out and run

I'll be back in a corvette convertible

I take the road over the mountains

making sharp curves at high speeds

across the yellow fields of summer

and through the cold gray beaches of winter

to settle in a place up north

where I paint little houses

and buy a little home.

They say the world is a rock.

And with a chisel

I carve my name in the stone.

Meat and potatoes

were served at the table

9 mouths and a roof to keep out the sky,

and parents that told us early and often

in this life you're on your own, and why...

First the business of life is handled

then the joy of free time is earned,

along with the meat and potatoes

a valuable lesson was learned.

So I balanced me work and me play

and betters been the use of me time,

the heavy lifting for me in the morning

and the rest of the day is mine.

When the last of me breath is taken

and I've used up all of me time

it's been work clothes for me in the mornin'

and the rest of the day is mine.

Today's

lovey dovey grandmas kill me

I remember my grandma

she was German and I don't know

if that had anything to do with it?

But one night she was baby sitting

and she wouldn't let me go to bed

till I knew my lesson cold. It paid off

with a sense of pride as the next day

when the teacher began with the questions

my hand was the first one that shot up.

The lesson was there is potential

inside of you if you go to the trouble to bring it out

there is a reward you can feel.

The lesson learned was

if you do the work…

good feelings will follow.

Treasure Hunting

I've made it this far, to lonely town

to walk these lonely streets without a name

The town watches and gives me a new name

there goes "the one who follows hopes and dreams ".

The way is hard, the way hopes and dreams are hard

to hold onto and the way they sound silly to own

The way they slip away, or you lose sight of and forget

true vision comes from the heart

Freedom is the spark to get it going

knowledge and experience I hold as lamps

hopes and dreams are fires I stoke

to keep life's real treasures

burning in my heart.

My pattern is set

rising before the sun seeking completion

taking this burden one step further

at noon I rest by the shores

seeking relief for an ache deep within

drawn to the deep blue mysteries and

the immense beauty before me

each blue and green wave that rises and falls

peaceful and calm, restless and relentless

my eyes full I'm reminded

of something undone, some failure,

some of many things I cannot do,

pulled away and back to town

cussing and leaving a mark

everywhere I go.

Found this in the trash

with the leftovers from the race

between what you want or can't have

Ambition charges the gate

all freedom and roses

clothed in hand me down beliefs

of the old whose lives go round and round

Pray to an image on a stone

wear this cross for protection

fill up the empty rooms with

science, education and facts

Music blares harsh lyrics and pounds a beat

shouting admission for a dollar

Love is open arms with nets

shiny lures and hooks

Thieves troll open waters

with false advertisements

giving directions to broken down hotels and empty suburbs

The wild animal gets caught

in a trap of its own making

Time escapes like a punctured raft

and through the waste basket of your heart

the loneliest person emerges

and finds something with no strings

and a warning label that reads

Beware there are a lot of fakes out there,

the pure heart of the child

is the only thing worth keeping

All the rest is trash

but it was no sin to try.

Desire

Rivers of desire

like wind that cannot be held

I feel you all the way

down roads with no end.

I saw a child running

late to class such a happy clod,

You or I much too serene and deep

We have a more difficult trip to make

the harder path toward self-discovery,

across the country to the sea

learning to be satisfied with little

calling little a lot

handling disappointment, being thankful

loving in a random way,

Please stay where I can find you

in yellow fields anchored under blue skies

where my lines can find you,

should you find anything utilitarian, please share,

We may have to change

because of you I sing.

Falling for you like rain

like winter rains that fall steadily

all night long, mightily at times

soaking the ground and the days

and days like the pages of a thick book,

stacks and piles of lonely nights by the fire

that burns to keep you warm and give you light,

Hurting like the work that must be done

and how quickly time passes taking everything

in its path like fire, hurting like the distance between us

and whatever you need I can look for

and bring home to keep you happy,

hurting like waiting for spring

and waiting so long for heart's desire,

stacking up the piles of pages

near the fire, to keep the fires burning

through the winters,

till all the rain has fallen

and everything has burned

thinking like this

at 1:27 am.

One night

while I lay sleeping

yellow wildflowers started popping up

everywhere filling the bed spilling onto the floor

racing to the window, down to the garden

and in one direction only

beating a path directly to your house

then climbing the wall

in through the window

across the floor

and jumping up into and

filling your bed

where you lay sleeping

until finally,

at last

we shared the same dream.

The wind breathed upon me

and brought these lines for a song

there you were close to me

just like you belong

We walked together

once again

just like we were in love

seeing me as I see you

whatever happens next

is enough

If you feel it

you can stay

if not

just walk away

Even if you leave

you won't be far away

I'll remember you like a dream

I'll remember you like a song

and you'll be here with me

here with me

I'll remember you like a dream

I'll remember you like a song

and you'll be

here with me

I like the feeling

when the warm wind blows

and the sound that rustles trees

branches start to sway and lose their leaves

everyone knows it's gonna to rain

Hurry up and get inside

by the window look outside

that's how it is don't ask me why

everyone knows it's going to rain

Hope this change in the weather

that turns a stream into a river

turns your feelings for the better

and makes this dream

come together

Falling steady

all night long

soothes my soul

just like a song

on the roof, it's coming down -hard -now

I say your name to hear the sound

Stay up late if I have to

one light in the house still on

I wish I had the breeze that carried you along

all I have is a song.

I wish I had the breeze that carried you along

all I have is a song.

Every day I pass you from the other side

I try to speak but say nothing

as you keep walking right on by

I open my mouth to speak

but my tongue feels like a brick

the words I want to say

get stuck and don't make the trip

I don't know how to go on

when so little seems to change

everything in your world

seems to mock and cause me pain

Could be prayer is working

and these ways are wise I keep

cause everything I do leads me back

to this quiet house

where I make my bed and sleep.

I give you a page

that always needs

to be filled with pain

that never leaves

even God can't fill

what this hunger needs

a face and a name

and love that breathes.

From sunrise to moonlight

follow the music that collects on the water,

open the chest that holds all the dreams

share your favorite songs

till the river runs dry, till the river runs dry

Just keep going till morning for no other reason

than the one you keep in your heart.

Determination

Leave notes on trees

where once grew leaves

to delight the wanderers

Don't walk downtown,

too sad

nada nada

Make music

stay out late

get tattoos

till you run out of skin

Congo the bongos

keep the beat

as long as you can.

It's a song of six wild rivers

that you can't hear

tall miles of forest that only speak green

with ears that can't hear you cry

It's the Trinity Alps and the Kings Mountain Range

with names like God that try to pass for a friend.

It takes time

like those rocks

that stand against the beating waves

for you to see the beauty

like the naked lady in the surf

who wants a man who can build her a house.

It'll be a long foggy night

before you get a foothold

hope you got some grit in that backpack homie

cause you're on your own.

At Disneyland

there was a chain link fence that protected the Disneyland property. Papers and trash collected along the base. A narrow strip of hard packed dirt and not particularly manicured landscape provided a slight buffer from the busy highway. Welfare kids from a rundown motel nearby played unattended. A tough breed of homeless scrounged and begged in the motel parking lot. At night, it felt like a robbery could happen. Same with Santa Monica Pier. A guy with red eyes was fishing. Something in his face set him lower than the tourists. The view was still beautiful as gray waves lapped at the iconic shores. The place for the muscle men was still there but where Paul Anka and Annette shake out their blanket is only in your mind.

The idyllic time has passed but pastimes remain. Closer to your own hometown they're still there with whatever toys you have and whatever entertainment your imagination can find. When does the golden age of innocence wear off? When your friend takes a serious paper route or when reviews from the first high school dances come in?

Do they have anything like that in Russia? China, Finland or England where the beautiful sea meets the hard-crusted edge of humanity? Like Brighton Beach or Coney Island or Rye Beach or Far Rockaway?

And then in the night you take a horse and leave. The next day you meet up with a hobo and your second education begins. You ride hard with a serious wind at your back and reach the other shore. Your eyes open wide and can't wait to dive in. Everything at once. The apartment, a job, a girl and friends. You want to write home but you don't know who to send it to or where to begin. You're not sure what you've found but you have a willingness that burns like fire.

Holidays, birthdays, rainy days, Mondays, good days and bad days all roll into one. Your old favorites don't work anymore. Don't satisfy and you can't put it together. You know what it takes but you don't seem have it. It seems impossible but you don't even think of quitting. It becomes a way of life. Then one day you look back and realize this feeling has taken you a long, long way.

Inspiration

See all the blue

around the yellow grass

waving like a man?

See the sun

laying down on the water

shimmering in the wind

Feel the wind blowing

across the gray sand like a song

Like a song of the song

of the man of the man in me

with daylight in his hands.

I try to keep it simple

you are above me

so, I try harder

when faced with difficulty

I remember how huge you are

when I think I've lost everything

I consider how big everything is

when in darkness

you come on quiet as day

when I'm filled with fear

I borrow the faith I need

when uninspired

I remember how short life is

and how much time has passed.

How much I want you

is a love fire burning

I see in you

all that is beautiful and amazing

I hope for you.

Whatever I find I share

all I have I give

nothing is ever lost

only gained.

I get up early

and welcome the sun because how many free days does a man have?

The sun tries to shine from the east but rain has already fallen

the weather is uncertain.

A thick cloud bank lays on the western edge of town.

I look for inspiration

and a rainbow appears in the midst of the clouds.

A trigger had been pulled and I begin to run.

I believe God has the day off but has left his music on.

I slow down a second to feel the love.

For everyone still with you

and the door open a little for those who are not

then to live your life like nobody cares and for those who do

you grow together in this light, in a garden as friends.

Day ends and I enjoy the night recalling the moments

one by one, like stars that come out and light up inside.

Things I find beneath the tree

more colorful than the bows and wrappings

of Christmas packages

Memories of loved ones who've climbed mountains

with the grace of bighorn sheep,

Friends who gathered like a herd of thirsty elk

to drink from a silver pond

The wild horse freedom of the last day of school

and the open range

A sea of golden fields laid out before me waving invitations

Mountains of puff clouds stacked up on the horizon

like the full upper decks of stadiums cheering

Young oaks I meet along the way

who climb yellow hills just to see what they can see,

a cereal bowl of coco leaves we pick through like baby spinach

making our heads light and dizzy and,

A hard, hard rain that falls me to sleep

puts my dreams in color, with friends and

in a thousand other crazy scenarios

filling my heart with wonder cheering hard for life.

Better to keep going

with our lives

There's enough chores and demands and aging.

If you find pleasure in quiet hours

when everyone else is filled with their own amusements

then the kingdom

is not so bad

and the travels bring joy

as fear takes a back seat

without any say in the music.

I'm open to

favorable winds

westward trains

little surprises...

the slow progress

of the work at hand

quiet nights and rain.

Notes from July

on the Painting Page

felt my knee squish

and play like an accordion

then stuck my brush

in the wrong color paint

On my mind

a girl in Jamaica

She's every color

of the rainbow to me.

Healing

From rough conditions

and shaky starts

comes hardy growth

But how can you force friendship or love?

Some fields won't produce

so why take the time to sow?

Walking in sunshine

in the middle of the day

by the blue blue waters

where the river meets the bay

Time is a river

and all things are mine

like the diamonds on blue water

in the noon sunshine

By the blue blue waters

the place I like to go

it doesn't cost a thing

when the healing waters flow

the ducks and egret gather

with the piper and the crow

down by the river

when the healing waters flow

It'll cure whatever ails you

You can let your troubles go

by the blue blue waters

when the healing waters flow

Hurting

like a kid playing in the dirt

when his friend had to go

you have to pet your heart softly back to health

sing to it softly, losing the tune

till the song comes back to you

Pruning the dry leaves trimming the dying parts

a fortunate weed does better

in the sun, if you pamper yourself

with healthy thoughts

till health returns

till new rains come

sending confidence down to the roots

and back up into the currents

where new life is.

Love Covers All

There's a big difference

in the rush of time

people in a hurry

aren't very kind

But someone holds the key

that opens up the door

where healing waters flow

and love can be restored

Our differences are few

And travels take us far

We're still held together

There's a string from heart to heart

When you feel the love

the healing oil is poured

Do you think like me

that we could love once more?

When you feel the love

do you think of me?

When I feel the love

I still think of you.

Our differences are small

they don't matter anymore

cause when you feel the love

Love-covers-all.

Faith

I begin the day

head on my arms

leaning on the deck rail

gathering strength

like a prayer

Listen

to the wind calling

where the river bends

get out of the boat there

walk bold

in that direction

make your fire

here tonight

plant your corn

there tomorrow

Everything true

and in a row

You've changed the world already

now Golden Fields can grow.

Most days

walking the dog

or wherever I go, painters

being painters speculate

on how I could improve this house

Sometimes I offer counsel

how owners could do it themselves

and regret that I probably couldn't get to it

Those who could afford it I pass on

for other reasons, it's a people thing

mostly but I do get roped in on things

I'd like to have missed

I like to come away with the feeling

I stole a small bag of gold

or else leave a blessing where I laid my hands

on some random soul, some random soul

passed my checklist met my conditions

for outreach, then I package the effort

along with those that didn't go so well

and send them down the well of good hope

where good outcomes flow

for you and me, painting and otherwise.

I believe in the living word

carried on the breath of man

where two or three are gathered

in the midst, there I am

I am in the sunrise on the summit

and the fog that burns off by ten

I am in the mist that clings to the valley

and the sunlight that filters through the trees

I am always with you and will never leave.

Days roll out

like a railroad track

all go forward

and none go back,

they wind and turn

towards the setting sun

may you safely get there

when the work is done,

So, sow good seeds

pray kept from harm

till it all comes up

on a Golden Farm.

Friends and Others

My friends

a tea string

holds us together

I would have it something

much stronger.

See all the blue

around the yellow sun

touching someone

waving its hand

breathing like a man?

Many under the same sun wane

feeling the same,

from your heart

pour yourself out

on some fertile spot

close enough

to be a friend

for the music it made.

Whan a sparrow falls

I think prayerfully

and feel for them.

I send my feelings out

on prayer ships

to search the seas.

I pull their faces up

resurrecting them

from old days.

I put their faces

on smoke columns

that rise from September's fallen leaves

filled with the incense

of tree lined streets

where they grew.

I put their faces

on tireless thought clouds

that search heavens and earth.

If one of these sparrow friends should fall

hands full of fond memories

are there to catch them

and lift them up till they feel the wind

and strength returns

to the wings of their falcon heart

and they are ready to fly again.

The room may be empty

but my heart is full,

I like it like this

quiet holding onto my energy

Every minute that passes I drink like wine

My friends I hold you here like wine.

I need you as much

as the food, air, and water of life

to me you are the wine.

I walk, work, and live to be with you again

you are always on my mind.

I savor your memory like wine.

You are the food, air, and water of my life

I feel you like the sun that shines the vibration you give

I receive and give you mine.

To me you are the wine.

It's quiet now

and quieter still my heart

like father and mother

for a few hours tonight all will be well

and no great thing will be done,

I don't need great, just peace and health

as long as I can

not too rich or poor,

just enough...

There are many I truly love

sprinkled on my life like spice

For those I'll use up my strength

and last word.

Most people pass

right on by

or stay a night and go,

if you decide to enter

don't close the door,

I love to see

your sunshiny face

held by a string,

take you everywhere

I go and keep the future

open ended.

My friend the ocean

all can find you

there you are in gray, green or blue,

Why I place myself beside you,

your immensity and beauty

never fails I guess.

Your motion and rhythm soothe me,

 either way you're always there

just like a friend

I can find you.

If you don't spill any

there should be enough

you get the last hit

while the bee still has buzz

while the garden holds colors

and the peaches have fuzz,

Before the rain falls

in the dry creeks and the banks overflow

before we had anything to do

or anywhere to go

before little things became big things

and took us away

our hearts were green fields

where we used to play.

After a long drive

from Hopi Nation on the Second Mesa we make it to Bobby-land

just in time for sunset and cooling temps. I make my way across the

front yard and notice two or three gray rabbits hopping around the

Arizona style landscape. At the front door, I see him through the glass and hear his welcoming voice. We hug and say things. Stand back, bro hug and shake again.

He talks. Same positive energy as always. You hear the New Jersey coming through but it's a man's voice not like when we were 20. He looks fit and doesn't run away with the conversation. What do you want to do he seems to be asking at every turn? Introductions are made and he offers us something to drink and we accommodate the dog with a slow walk down the street, a ' paseo ' passing a two-time Super-Bowler's house. I remark to Bobby the colors of the sunset, the crescent moon and desert landscape look like a Carlos Castaneda book cover.

Over dinner with his wife Cathy and son Jarrod and girlfriend Page we talk of things old and new as good feelings are exchanged all around. As the night goes on you wish you weren't tired and didn't have a ways to go before we reach the hotel. It's not like the old days instead we come away refreshed and glad my friend and his family are doing well.

He found an old picture of me from back in the day and offered it to me. I said no you keep it and if you break out these pics again, if somebody else comes through, I want to be remembered as part of the crew.

I saw my neighbor approaching with his dog early in the morning walking. And I moved away and made room and from across the street shouted and waved a greeting, And I said today I am working, and then tomorrow I'm working, and then after that something bigger. And he said that's great and good luck. And I said yes and waved and he waved and we went our ways. Cause we're neighbors and wish each other well.

Paul the roof estimator came by.

We had a great conversation.

Went off topic.

Talked about everything.

Every sentence punctuated with the f bomb.

Really easy to talk to.

He said he was a bartender.

I could see that.

That he loves people.

Does that pass for Christian love?

Cause these are the easiest people to love.

My Good World

has someone at home

who lets me be

a bright spot,

keeps her side of the room warm

and a bright spot that I need,

sheltered and safe

where I am loved and adored

even worshipped and obeyed

by my cat and dog

Godlike royalty I imagine my neighbor

with his moon god

and pot tree, no,

let him be

just a neighbor

in my good world.

I saw a house

that could use some paint

I could fix that with the colors of spring,

the owner with dyed hair and red glasses

would be happy and the house will sing,

The girl at the market's tattoo that

peeked out from the edge of her sleeve,

to flirt or joke with someone

but today she just gave change.

The pet store owner was nice

and carried my food to her chest like a baby,

The city worker waived traffic through

and I continued on as I pleased

like a stray cat who comes and goes

Who we see around in the alley

but for the rest nobody knows.

For the stars

someday I'll write a book

a face goes on each page

for the stars in my life

where ' all the world's a stage'

the people who stand out

in the places that I go,

ordinary people

I hardly even know

they seem to take me as I am, they

help me make it through,

in the story of my life

there'll be a page for you.

Meet Me in the Valley

I'm dreamin' of the old days

can you tell me where they've gone?

my heart keeps going back there

to the streets of my hometown.

I don't know where the time went

but the memory isn't far

so, meet me in the Valley

on a seat at Dillon's Bar.

Meet me in the Valley

Like the days when we was young

we'll stay out all night drinking

fall over when we're done

Meet me in the Valley

we'll see who comes along

tell the good old stories

play all the favorite songs

Meet me in the Valley

cause time keeps rollin' on

so meet me in the Valley

on the streets of our hometown.

Meditations

My soul escapes

searching the dark blue night

and beyond, far beyond stars

In the purple silence

waking I take my piece of sun

and go where music plays.

Move along

with the morning light

let the flocks of words fly by

Mix in with the songs

of the Old Souls

keeping rhythms

of home and heart.

Before me

the ordinary nameless people of the town

I silently applaud

I adapt the patience of a green field

and follow the music

of a gentle stream

to dwell in the far and broad reaching

happiness of a sunny afternoon

moving easily through the day

saying thank you to everything.

Dreamt of a house built in the 40's needing paint

I'm standing on the grounds across from the horse pen

moving ladders thinking of my dream lover

hoping she will be pleased with my efforts.

I think about my eyesight and how much longer

I can see? I'm thankful for my hearing and wonder

whether or not God will speak strong enough and clear enough

to make a difference?

I'm lucky to have this life and the one I think about.

Up early- cats get fed before they whine, bathroom and get coffee

started. This is a quick move I've mastered without tripping over the

pet gate. The dog noses the back door, he can get bossy too.

I'm trying to keep it quiet somebody's sleeping. Socks on first but

the feet get cold on the tiles. At the back door, a thick fuzzy moonlit

fog lays down on us all. I still can't believe I live here.

Read my FB replies now try to write something. Put some color in it

like pastels in print. Cook something up. It might be out of a can but

I'll rinse off the dishes and leave them in the sink. I'm not a total

loser.

I hear the bed creak. A body makes its last turn before the alarm.

What a difference somebody else breathing inside the same four

walls makes. Two quiet souls under one roof. We're not a tragic

mess. They're out there in the eerie fog. Made a wrong turn

somewhere. Probably so minor at the time they didn't even notice.

The druggies, thieves, mental, the homeless, they're out there.

Keeping it real. Making this even more special.

We were young

and beautiful

but we don't understand

the other measure of beauty

In time

we change

and if you keep your looks

that's fine

but the other measure of beauty

starts to shine through

and that one is true.

I spend these cool summer mornings on the deck when the gray sky

first appears. The domestic animals begin to stir and the birds begin

their song. Can you blame them for singing early with such short

lives?

The vines are thick and alive as an orchestra of birds announce their

pleasure. Then swooping and diving towards the bird feeder,

hopping from limb to the feeder stand, pushing and shoving,

laughing and mocking one another for hogging the seeds.

There is the hum of an engine up the street as work begins for some.

I look up at 3 or 4 birds gathered by the birdhouse I put near the top

of the clothes pole. I installed it at some risk to my safety and I

thought I did something wrong. It looked cute and natural but I gave

up and thought they didn't like it.

That teaches me something about my life, my small efforts and my

work. These mornings are like nails that hold my life in place and

bring me its song.

Be the steady character

in this slow drama grounded by those natural elements

time, weather, seasons,

As purposeful flesh and blood as rivers that flow

wanting from some wishing stone

one star to follow.

A lonely couple hours pass

lay down beside me

like an old moon I've known

days and nights spin

like tires on miles of road ahead

each one a missing friend

this unguarded moment

fills with the quiet song of rain

an animals soft cry

gives wings to its wild form

and in the wind above the high ridge

seeks a peaceful blue star.

November's chill fog lapping at the doors

inside the warmth of fires and cabernet

channel surfing for peace

not every turn unlucky,

Toss up those soft pitches

that leave the park,

Fill the empty box cars

that ramble through the night

passing by the honest farms

Where every house is lit

by yellow light,

and on every pale colored wall

shadows dance

and every room is warm.

I am the foundation,

framing and substance

that lies beneath the style

I have wheat, corn, and flour,

honey, meat and cloth,

outside the wood is cut and stacked for winter,

I walked through summer collecting berries,

my perch is high in a strong tree

my thought children are blue robin's eggs

nesting in branches near my heart

an army of thousands watches alongside

my heart trusting like a kitten

curled up on a blanket

purring her meditations

I shall allow

these questions

that arise

like a pesky fly

trapped by the window

where it fights for freedom

And when I come to a breach

in the road like this

look beyond,

Till streams of thought flow

like rivers

that reach a quiet pasture

and lay down like cattle

and wonder why does the beautiful sun

set so late?

What do I want as May slips through my fingers?

A new starting place where the old rug remains.

Who is a hero like me that will take on Monday?

It's a sad lot to consider that those beauties from youth

who used to make our heart stop,

where are they now that it beats so easily and strong?

In the silence that I like to pass my time

wandering from thought to thought like new towns

I haven't been to before.

Thoughts weave into a blanket of comfort

and a pillow to lay my head on.

Because for all the stress and angst, and noise there is peace.

No cable, phone or internet

just satisfying peace I can reach

where only the most beautiful things exist

when I close my eyes and sleep.

The stuff down here

that's pretty good

when it all comes together nicely

and the times when it starts to come together

and then falls apart

there's a spirit of beauty behind it

and one day that's all there will be.

The old man tested the weather and soon felt the warm sun upon

him. He slouched in his chair and pulled his cap down to shield his

eyes letting the sun kiss his cheek and work over the rest of his body.

The rushing noise around him was it part wind and part traffic? To

him it sounded more like a river. He wished his heart could expand

to include all the missing parts of his life but here he was in

Humboldt County and his imagination could only carry him so far.

He thought the best place to be at this moment would be on the north bank of the Klamath in the sun with his back up against a tree. Wear your favorite jeans and hoodie and fall asleep with your head on my lap if you like he thought.

If you have to beg or promise big things to get someone to come along with you is it really worth it? And those who would come that's fine but does that make your heart complete? He thinks the country will never get its act together and that too is very sad but that's not the thought he's looking for either.

As the last hours of afternoon pass on what feels like the first day of Spring a bird trills from somewhere in the trees. Our ears perk up at what sounded like a twig crack behind us. A part of him hopes it is something big. Moments of stillness pass and all he hears is the sound of a squirrel digging into the bark and working his way up a tree.

He did everything he knew to make his life better. How did he know it would all lead to this?

My 3rd Job

Vietnam don't count.

besides this was a fresh start

collect unemployment and work for cash

with Ralph the Gardener.

Good hard work outdoors

in the spring, it's cold in Jersey

cleaning up yards

raking lots of leaves in tarps

hauling them over our backs

Like Santa to the big truck.

He'd come by at 10am with a 6 pack.

There were 3 of us

that meant Andre and John got two each.

I was dizzy on a beer at 10am.

so, you worked your ass off

for 25 dollars, a day.

and that was good money

Then for lunch Andre

(who we called a "greenhorn")

had a huge hunk of cheese

big as a softball

and a half loaf of Italian bread

like a junior football

and that other beer.

Then payday Ralph would forget if you worked 5 days or 4

and try to pay you for 4.

Then I went to work for Ron a German guy

on Gregory Av. and he worked his ass off too.

Led by example.

It was summer now and sweat would just drip off his nose

as he pushed that lawnmower.

Jimmy O'Malley worked for him too.

6 days a week it was like that,

then Ron would clean up after a no let up Saturday

and shoot down the shore and hit the bars

and tell us Monday morning how he met one gal who was ok

in a not so excited voice, I may call her he said,

and then next week the same thing.

It was good hard clean work.

I thought about that today as I was eating

a baked potato for lunch. Just microwaved

it 5 1/2 minutes and threw it in the back of the truck

and it sat there next to the tools all day

just like that and ate it and thought of Andre.

Recycling

turning over and over

the things that worked before will work again

those lessons at the core of 2017 and before

the peelings and green leaves not wanting to waste

Turning over and over

layering in a mix of hindsight and conscience

undertaking a partnership with heaven and earth

gambling against pestilence and drought

with abundance and favor in mind

Hands hold the smooth handle of the spade

spread evenly across the dark soil

both hands starting to believe

having the feel of blessings in them

acting like two fresh lit prayer candles

flickering on a winter night.

Love

A vineyard of red wine

I the Lord do keep

I will water it every moment

and keep it

day and night.

Isaiah 27

Plant yourself

a sweet vine

keep it for yourself

hold it like a baby

love for all it's worth

One that can't be stolen

your precious time

on earth.

You may never understand

why I burn

lean into the fire

and gaze

with quiet wonder

Like a smooth stone

hold the warmth and tell me

your stories,

your burning version of the truth

I so need you here

where the road has led

from where I come and go

at the edges of the earth.

Happy Valentine's

I hated this day. Like I needed a reminder of what I'm missing? Like the other 364 I haven't been looking? Adding more pressure to make a move you're not ready for with someone who isn't right for you. I mean biology would say you're ready at age 14 but society would say something different. Society says a lot of things ...

I used to struggle with feelings of self-worth. That was before I understood that true self-worth comes from being able to do something well. By achieving little success over and over confidence grows. Being able to take care of yourself, being able to see a good future for yourself are the qualities of a leader.

Leaders look into the future and see and think what they'll need. Then they prepare to make things right to carry out that vision. Once you've convinced yourself you have a future then make your move.

Before you ask someone to come along with you, you should have something to point to. Something you can believe in. If you are believable they might be willing and they might be the right one for

you.

That's what dating and flowers and dancing and chocolates are all

about. Finding someone who believes in you.

W ore out

many a pair of shoes

favorite t-shirts and jeans

till I found you,

who took me in

broken

like my boots

gave me back

to myself

standing tall

looking good.

Sometimes puppies get sick

born not right for this world

the doctor explains there's no cure

kittens sometimes have three legs

and need special care

people get cancer

and that's why there is love.

My love

has this quiet little life

with names for all the alley cats

Or the old farmers who

live miles from the city,

she visits once a month

who so could use the help,

And then she takes my soul

and holds it up, soul to soul

and loves it like a three-legged kitten.

My love checks on Coco

Lewis couldn't boil an egg he says,

"please, make her a meal, I'll pay you ".

Coco gets her favorite meal

soft because her dentures aren't fitting right

Lewis doesn't pay a thing

and I get another lesson on love.

Our Love

takes many forms

early before day breaks

before the jewels of morning sparkle

it visits and travels like the foreign ships that come and go

the men unload their cargo and the fishing boats

go to sea

Our love is a trail we follow with vistas

where we write new chapters

Our love is the pretty colors

of the orange marigold and purple

of a careless summer garden,

In a family of birds chirping

and in the pleasing, sounds of footsteps

on a gravel path we take,

Our love is heavy and it bends the ends of oak boughs

and is in the tips of branches

reaching as far as they can go,

Our love is in different dreams passing one another

only a few of which we share. So many dreams

my heart cannot contain the dreams of all the people.

A bird I know flies away, I want to tell her something

So bad my heart explodes,

A tear forms in my eye

whether it is from love or cold

I cannot tell

Our love

takes many forms...

For now

let's follow the scent

of the baker's baking bread

he gets up early and bakes his bread with love.

It seems every one of our senses tells us

We are made to feel the love.

And it (love) never stops flowing

like a river, it leads, it follows

it comes up behind you

and sweeps you away for awhile

and keeps going,

always taking you further and further

You have to remember

you are here where you are now for love

and go wherever love takes you,

follow it downstream like a river,

into the crooks and crannies,

along the levees down into the eddies,

whatever you find love has led you to,

to the tadpoles the guppies and minnows…

the small fish are people too.

Read an obit today

Of a man who lived to be 90 and was married four times. Married

early, his first divorce left him with nothing. He moved and

remarried. A serious accident disabled him and then another divorce.

Then his next wife died. After a " very lonely period " he met his last

wife. Of his last wife, it was said " she was truly the love of his life;

his love was 100% unconditional ... he knew her better than anyone

ever could...he cared for her with such love and tenderness. Though

he was diagnosed with cancer and given 6 months to live he lasted

15 months because " I do not want to leave Allie alone in this

world." How unpredictable life can be for some. He was a multi-

talented man with varied interests that led him to action. Above all

how necessary to have one person to love and I wrote this note.

To My Lover

Don't tell me you're sick

cause I wouldn't want to live without you

don't tell me you're doing well

cause I might feel small and unnecessary

don't tell me how much you love me

cause I might stop trying

Just hang in there with me and we'll go through this together

enjoying the comfort, we bring to each other

Don't stay away too long

I might sink too low in despair

don't pretend you're a casual friend

that's not who you are

you are the pilot light to my life that must always stay lit

in a world too cold we click- and always have fire.

This is what it comes to

lying on the couch

window open and slightest breeze

that moves the curtain reaches me

The sound of the plastic wheelbarrow

on the concrete that no one commands

my love at work in the garden she loves

Whatever you don't force or command

like friendship or love

like the living breathing sky

that flows through the curtain

is poetry that touches me.

November rains

trace the sides of empty houses

the old days long gone

return over and over

The wind says " storm "

and life bends to an uncertain future

I want you to know

I share the same fear

of darkness and night

Feel the same sadness

with loss and the passing of time

I want you to know

I took care of all the little things

while you were gone.

I want to be the soil

on your hands and knees

from working in the garden that you love.

The roof that keeps you dry from rain above.

I want to be the quiet street you exit and retreat.

The air of friendly manner towards the neighbor that you greet.

The heat that rolls through your house on a cold winter's day.

The random feeling that comes from nowhere that makes your day

A part of what brings you joy and never gives you pain.

And the air down deep in your lungs

after a long walk on a country lane.

I had a dream or two

I watched them fall through

till you came along

turned the sky to blue

I was down and lonely

that's when you showed me

life needn't always be so hard

that this might be a good time

and this might be the right place to start

All I had to do

was speak the truth

let the feelings from my heart come out

Unbelievable

that's what you are

Unbelievable

a real-life superstar

one who I can trust

that means so much

giving me feelings that fly

Miraculous and wonderful

remembering and wondering

where was this strength I find?

Life needn't always be that hard

dreams shouldn't always be that far

this might be a good time to start

All I had to do

was speak the truth

let these feelings of my heart

come out

Unbelievable

that's what you are

Unbelievable

a real-life superstar

one in a million

and dream come true

who lets me be me

by you just by being you

We started to do things I never did before.

Take vacations. Eat meals together. Get a pet.

Enjoy life around the house. Fix it up. Plant a garden.

Be there for each other.

I helped her through school. She helped me through life.

The earth is the Lord's

and the fullness thereof

if I make my bed in hell

I can't escape,

So He sent me an angel

with an angel's face

to help me bide time and ease pain

And treasure she's been

like a pearl of great price

and I've never been poor again

Success

The wind whispers outside our chill abode

November Taos moon lights a dog's chilly path

who finds his way without whimper or complaint

I am tumbleweed, sagebrush, cactus and pine

but in the wind moon peace

I am reservation stray, sleep and grace.

Our birthdays serve as milestones

for the years we have traveled

we tend to stay on familiar paths

and don't get often lost

do familiar things

and return to the same house

it's what works best

our minds and experience tell us

take care

because we want to be there

for more good moments

trips, experiences, birthdays, holidays

vacations, promotions,

You're hopeful

life and civilization

are set up to accommodate you

to make things run smooth

for yourself and others

to get what you want and need

our birthdays are milestones where

our bodies tell us what they still can or cannot do

we were made to be hopeful

from birth till the day we're through.

It is good

that we ache in both bone and limb

from our efforts,

the day was well spent

It is the spirit that suffers most.

Our effort was strong

creating and building

the beauty which is our lives,

Our energies depleted

our bodies united in common fatigue,

Resting on the mismatched chairs

of our budget, we take the same foods

our mothers have made

on the kiln dried hand painted pottery

that reflects the land where we stand,

Reminding us and grounding us

in our beginnings and our ends,

where we come from and what is true,

Nothing is lacking and yet we are not complete.

We use the simple hand tools of our forebears

each one well suited for the task

to pick up and continue where they left off,

bearing this gift

to carry on as we see fit,

It is good that we tire

when skin touches skin,

and feet touch feet,

for our effort was strong

our sleep and dreams will be sweet

and still we hunger and thirst

for our life is not yet complete.

Success Is like

the truck

you spend all Saturday afternoon

cleaning and polishing

hoping Sunday inspiration will hit

you'll get in the truck and cruise

and like the river flow

but it's a truck and you have to drive

trust your built- in navigation

start out in that direction

miles and miles blow by

without much change in scenery

until you notice flowers start popping up here and there,

then everywhere all around

like the back yard in June

and good times keep fallin.

When I paint farmhouses

out in the country on a sunny day

I am most happy. Two horses are

nearby in a field, a blonde one and a red one who watch me work

and come when I call and they are like

my friends. I feel my strength as I move

around in both the sun and the shade and this

adds to my pleasure. At some point the pretty lady

of the farm asks me if I'd like something to drink

and I take a soda and nurse it through the day

enjoying her kindness. It's a good day to think of

my dream lover and today she's sarcastic and playful.

The day goes by quickly and feel by the sun in the sky

it's quitting time and put my gear off to the side.

On the way home, I roll down the window and think that

my dream lover is happy too. If I could whistle I would

but driving with the window down is just as good.

"You're pitching", Tony said.

Little League, Babe Ruth and High School

I thought about semi pro for a minute

but that'd be too hard

it would take thousands of pitches

just to get ready, so I threw it into the sea of

"you'll never know".

Turns out I needed that arm

for holding sanders against walls

trying to get a smooth feathered edge

for hoisting ladders and 5 gallon cans

fingers that threw a pretty good curve

now squeezed caulk guns all day

and carried 3 one gallon cans at a time

to save time cutting to the bone

at night fall asleep on their own

Daddy said I'd learn the hard way

but it was my way and the best thing about it is

loading up the truck after another job done

check in my pocket heading down the road

to happy-happy land

just like walking off the mound with a "W "

in the Big Leagues of my life.

My soul and body

cooperating. Maybe this spring

I will get to work early

and take off late?

It's all out there waiting

backdrop and inspiration.

Maybe someday the spirit will fall

creating the perfect American.

One you can be proud of and take pictures of.

The hardest part is doing your work

and staying healthy.

If you've made somebody's highlight reel

don't disappoint.

Travel well.

Make your mother proud.

Keep bringing back days winning.

Spirit

God help the little man

in the room thinking hard

trying to write something beautiful

and the rain starts to fall

and starts coming down hard

keeps falling and laying down hard

on his roof and he thinks

the Lord is in that sound

and he writes of the beautiful sound.

Someone right now

could be walking

in that alley I was blest in.

I wonder if they feel it?

There isn't a shrine or a sign

just tire paths and garbage cans,

and weeds on the narrow road me and the dog walk

on, free and happy. I could give it a name

but tomorrow the blessing could fall

somewhere else and they would miss it.

It's good

that you have obvious flaws

so that others can relax around you

it makes them feel strong

Or that they know nothing about you

Then, when you speak

they hear nothing but spirit.

Fly little butterflies fly

from this cave behind the ribs

cheery and cherry faced soldiers

Stay true to your mission

and carry this message,

stay spaced apart and safe

you're all I've got

Be quick and skillful

and go for the heart,

Be brave my cherry faced friends

very brave putting yourself at risk

You little ones who are my feelings

special chosen ones set free to make this work

Only you do I trust to carry this message

that comes from my heart.

I am not the one

who speaks to the mountain

or calms the sea

Silence frames the thoughts that best calm me

By night they have rambled

and collected the logs

for the fires of my meditation

filling my dreams with flames

of what I want and who I love

The words I choose

are like smooth stones

beneath the fire still warm

They carry me through the day

like the hooves of graceful deer

beautiful as she moves

through woods or on rocky way.

If you find a piece of paper on the ground read enough to see if it

was meant for you.

When walking through the forest looking for wild animals

know that they only appear bringing their thrill when you

least expect it.

All night you dreamed of vivid characters and wild adventures.

Let the dream or prophecy come to you.

It may come as a little desert squirrel, stray dog or crow.

Or in the mornings red clouds jumping across the blue sky

like upstream salmon. Carry the new feeling forward.

When you get home write it down.

All good things in life add up.

With the excitement of discovery and wonder

send it out the window on a paper plane if you have to.

All good things in life are meant to be shared.

Remember "in the beginning was the word,

...and the word was alive, and the word was God".

If I could

I'd put these thoughts together

born on quiet nights

that travel like the sounds

of sad classical music coming from another room.

I'd send these thoughts

on the sleeping dreams of puppy dogs

quivering and chirping through

adventurous fields of night

as real as anything.

If I could

I'd send these peaceful thoughts

out as warm blankets

on the backs of night rider horses

galloping through the stars

If I could

these words

would chop down impossibilities

carve up obstacles

shake off fears

and conquer the world.

Having all and wanting more

of this soothing warm oil of love

I respect the idea that words can fly

and so rest believing they can.

What words will I choose

to allow to cross my lips?

What pleasant sounds

can I place

on open wounds

to bloom like flowers?

What cherries can

I place in the hands of others?

What tears can I collect

on gold and silver plates

to present to the

Lord of Hosts?

And so it falls to me

to be this bridge

and carrier of peoples,

To break down walls

and give things their proper names.

Seasons

When this year is in the books

and the people

sing all the old songs

and promise a new heart

better than gold

As Spring rolls into September

sad page after sad page

just keep going

for no better reason

than the one you keep in your heart

Before the rage of a new week starts

and the loudmouths of the world

tell you how things are and how you should feel…

I try to find my own words for this

mild, quiet evening, the last one in May.

A man, a little man is flipping out inside

trying to get out, almost in tears,

crying in some struggle over something…

of what he isn't sure

or that isn't even here, or anywhere.

I'm tired, he's not.

The flowers which I don't know the names of are standing pretty,

the chard is doing well

all reaching for the sun which is dropping in my tired eyes now,

the slightest breeze cools my ears, and crazy children

are laughing and talking excited,

they could be the only ones at home in this world.

A dog is barking excited too, and there's a church bell chiming long slow gongs...a swarm of birds are chirping different breeds I take it by the sounds, fresh cut grass and the quiet calm and lack of adult voices...the little man inside could not ask for anything more.

Nights like this my dad would water his garden, the smallest backyard in New Jersey with his uncool shorts and shirt. If you bugged him he'd squirt you, the little man in him would laugh.

New Jersey's fine if you got a boat tied up in the Navesink, or Egg Harbor by the summer place and a primary home and a nice big lawn in the center of the state. Why would you plant a garden in such a small yard? Coming to terms with his place in life? Calming the little man in him? The little man in me, watering these flowers now, just like him, it all was meant to be somehow.

Christmas Eve

And I thought of mother and father always teaching us.

How they knew I wanted the world and how a person who expects too much will always be disappointed, so their best gifts were their teaching and example how to get up early and be efficient, get going with a quick step, watch where you're going.

To consider the bright days of youth a light burden How to settle into the peace of night with a family meal and a good TV show

How to enter into the restful satisfaction that comes with accomplishment and to grow in the confidence that comes from experience.

So, I thought this Christmas I don't want to go home again that being impossible but rather that this Christmas finds me living with the good sense that comes from experience still benefiting from the lasting gifts that were paid for and given in the daily acts of love, long after the bows, ribbons, and wrapping paper were torn off and thrown about the room and the contents of the package forgotten.

Happy with the smells of animals,

hay and fair foods the last night of the fair

was surreal for this hard day and age,

Riding off mood relaxed the sun setting

shining on the sides of red barns

casting its warm glow on quiet farms

we looked for ice cream on Main

As artful fingers

drew beliefs in melon shades and tones

across the sky

warming us to the bone.

We start our days

and days, and days, and days

walking. Winter lasts forever

not wanting to let go.

We've fought back hard

with white wine and baguettes

and a fire going in the cabin

still I promise myself

the first three days of spring

I will give to my soul.

We keep walking rainy, foggy, and cloudy

looking for something we can pick up

and latch our hearts onto

and spin, and spin, and spin

until soul and body cooperate.

Today he is definite.

He leads. I follow

His plans and directions clear.

The past and future woven together

till it all fits together nicely

and we walk like this

in total perfection.

We collect things

play with them awhile

put them away

where they add up

The unfinished project in the garage

The clothes you are wearing right now

The dirt under your fingernails

The people who call you by your first name

The randomness of it all

becomes part of the story you tell.

This rainy day

so near to Christmas

feels like home

no happy ending

just old hands

soft to touch.

We'll dig a little soon

in the garden and cut the grass

in the small yard with the little hill,

I'll do a little paint and fix up cause the old house

needs it now and then, and when it's all done

we'll take a little victory trip

with the little money we saved up

And when we return we'll

sit outside by the garden

On the long evenings of summer

enjoying a small little victory

a small little victory in a life of

small defeats, small setbacks, aches and pains

that we can endure. And when we're gone

what difference will it make?

Our little life.

Travels

I feel

the blue of the North

completely true,

The draw of the South

warm yellow and inviting

The fire red of the West

wild and free,

And the love

from the East

is gold

I carry

wherever I go.

There's a place I've known

on the Yellowstone

where morning sparkles a dance its own

like a happy schoolgirl making her way home

Where water looks and sounds like the bronze wrinkled hands

of a pianist renown sending solitary notes

downstream on wish boats of yellow leaves

Sage, orange and brown russet tones of autumn hold it together

bend and sigh for fallen trees and whisper through wooden flutes

where sparrows escape with melodies

Everything sweeps toward the snow- capped mountains

where we feel peace

Our hearts frame pictures and store them

on yellow pages of old books

next to the orange, sage, and golden memories.

Road Notes

It was raining when we left.

600 miles day one. I promised

myself I'd be good. My love has to do all the driving.

She's the one who brings the music to my life.

My license expired.

Somewhere in S. Humboldt

the low clouds and fog blur the lines

between heaven and earth.

Is it smoke, fog, mist or clouds that form little halos

and crown groups of children trees on a green hillside?

The rain comes in waves

brother and sister rain, fight and get over it rain

Our lives a marriage of gray skies and evergreen expectations.

Puff clouds pile on tops of mountains, a buffer

against hasty exits and retreats, cushions for those

who get too high or fall too hard. Old trees

stand guard on narrow passageways

We salute the old sentries of safe passage

A silver spoon road lays out its long handle in front of us

dipping into a deep dish of fog.

Downhill we can't go so fast as to lose ourselves,

discomfort and determination buckle us in

If you close your eyes you might miss something

like a deer crossing

And then like the grateful earth that always gives back

sends the rain ascending from where it came

into a blue, blue sky and down a green hillside

where the sun peeks through and lays down a swath of light.

Sometimes the road is good.

It's 9am

when we start out of Sedona. 5 days without tv or radio. We are traveling through time and making our own news. Only scenic rocks and autumn colored trees to report on. I'm the designated court stenographer and Slide Rock and Oak Creek make the cut and become noteworthy entries. On the cutting room floor are miles of Yucca and Joshua trees, the Desert Palms Mobile Home Park, a sketchy housing village and shabby collection of RV's on that hot flat stretch from Bakersfield to Needles.

Winding our way upwards out of Sedona towards Flagstaff this stretch of road reminds me of a trip over to Diamond Mill Pond cutting through rock into the higher elevations. You need a good vehicle to do this. Moods are like wheels, they turn and I'm starting to feel it.

Flat, high and yellow is the plateau now that looks like Kansas. The sky is azure blue and huge stretching from one corner of the eye to the other and Arizona rolls like this into New Mexico. We see signs for Winslow and I start singing that song. "Well I'm standing on a corner in Winslow Arizona, it's such a fine sight to see, take it easy...take it easy " my love says I'm out of key and I say no I'm in the key of H for happy. Happy is always in tune.

This is what I wanted. I call my friend Gus... "Gustavo" and Thomas... "Tomas" Frank is Paco. Some guys take to the road for money, I take to the road for fun, moods are like big wheels turning and sometimes the road is fun.

Trinidad

Richard Hugo said in Driving Montana "the day is a woman who loves you" but this one isn't bad either. This one's a blend of something necessary and something fun, a little work then a little run, up to Trinidad on a beautiful day. My dog pulls low and hard claiming the ground beneath him like a philosophy I try to live by. From the first look out to the sea my heart sheds weight as care after care drops off. Thanks go up as I take it all in. Though I've seen it a thousand times I'm still blown away. From the highest peak, I scan north to south. My footsteps on the path on the way down sound like taps of my fingers on my desk.

A family approaches with Golden Retriever off leash. Somewhat in panic the woman scrambles, no worries my bull terrier is a caramel apple on a stick. Dad passes casual saying "bonjour" like I should know French? Reflexively I reply bonjour. The youngest girl trails like a lemon that fell out of the picnic basket. Her skin sandalwood her hair a tangle of coconut, 10 years away from being a real French beauty. Her eyes try to understand my dog and stores away an image from a family vacation.

A bank of wild bluebells appears standing along the base of the trail like school girls would line a parade. I call them "my lady's eyes". The Pilot Rock piece de resistance beholds the bay. A rust colored covering of lichen sits like a prayer cloth on the back of her head. The nape of the neck of my lady is red. I imagine the faltering lighthouse on top as a crown. The sun lays tangerines on each of her shoulders as offerings. Stoic in her gaze, accepting and level as a sage, deep speaks to deep, her eyes fill with sea water. The bass rhythms of the blue play on and wash over our souls soothing long after we're gone.

I threw two stones in the Rio Grande

Then five more trying to reach the other shore.

They all fell short, plunked before they got there.

I dipped my hand in the Rio Grande

To say I tasted the cold clean water.

Tributes

My mom said

holding out a piece of apple she was slicing and peeling "here, have

some ". Sharing like I was an equal. Sharing low key with no strings

attached like you would a friend.

I think of her as a young woman before me. At work with her

girlfriends all giddy over the boys they had chasing them and the one

on the hook. How they stayed in touch over the years "girl's night

out", phone calls, bowling league, planned visits to each other's house. To keep their spirits up and to remember how it all came about I suppose and to keep that feeling alive of when they were young.

How dad told me to write home it cheers mom up to hear from you. Me? What do I have to say that would cheer somebody up? I'm struggling with young man issues in every way what can I say about that that will help her? It's just something you'll understand someday. How something in writing can do that even if it is full of struggle and difficulty. I remember when they got old and hardly left the house and one day I was out and saw a busy hot dog place on Rt. 22 and as I was ordering mine I thought maybe they would like one too and as we spread them out on the kitchen table I knew I had made a good decision. Now I just have memories. No more mom and dad to share with. You'll have to find another. That's how they would want it. That's how it all began. A slice of your life, pared and peeled, share it just like you would a friend.

MOTHER

I was home for the holidays and it was supper time. I was in "my

seat", the one I had all the time growing up with six other brothers

and sisters. Now with Dad's passing and only my youngest brother

and sister left in the house there were just us four. Mom was a frail

lady by this time with thick glasses. Her hands trembled as she took

her medicine parceled out carefully by my younger brother Jim

seated across from me. Certainly not the same woman who would

call us from the kitchen and take the hot meals from the stove

placing them on the table, now Jimmy did most of that. The food

was on the table and they were ready to dig in but for me this was no

ordinary meal. I was accustomed at this point in my life with the

church group I was with to pray before meals whatever words of

thanks came to my mind. This would be a departure for them and

maybe a bit uncomfortable but this was the time and I had to do

something. To just dig in we would lose this moment forever. I

needed to mark the significance of it and what better way than prayer? I bowed my head to begin but as I formulated my first thoughts my lips trembled and I sobbed as tears began to flow. I didn't even get a word out just tears and I thought that's the best kind of prayer anyway. If God can't see tears He can't hear words.

When I was 11 I saw my mother cry. From the front room as she saw the ambulance come to take her father away from her childhood home across the street. She knew then and felt then what I feel now. She gathered herself quickly to be strong as I gathered myself quickly now to be strong and so that the others would not be uncomfortable.

My mom had her first stroke in '86 and it was during the holidays. As it occurred it was nighttime and we were watching tv when she said she felt something was wrong. The ambulance was called. 6 men arrived. Two of them were talking about last night's game or other off the field issues. I wanted to see game faces. My father was elderly so I intervened. I searched for the man with leadership in his eyes and walked him over to my mother. My way of asking him to treat her like she was your mother. They put her on the stretcher and navigated their way down the staircase and out into the cold winter night.

We had a piece of furniture that served as a record player, perhaps an RCA, where the family records would be stored, among our collection was a song called "Charlie My Boy" which Mom would sing along with. She made me feel special like that and I knew someday I'd have a beautiful wife because of the way she made me feel.

She would also sing along with the marching band for the high school football games that were played right up the street as well as some other songs we had in the house, "you've got to be a football hero, to get along with a beautiful gal". She would go through her yearbooks and I'd stop her and ask questions about the football and basketball players and she'd tell me who was good and what became of them. That was all the encouragement I needed. She stayed out of my business but I knew she was my biggest fan.

I let my grades slip in high school and had no intention of going to college. A day or two after graduation I was parked in front of the TV watching mid-morning shows when she came in and said, "you're not going to just sit in front of the tv all day. If you're not going to college you're going to get a job." That stung. And I did. And from that moment on I began to act like a man.

After Vietnam, I did landscaping and had a job at the Post Office. One day she read from the paper how they were looking for Sky Marshals. I got down to the Federal Building the next day and was one of the first round of recruits hired. She knew what kind of job I would respond to. It was a type of undercover work providing security for the airlines. As a result, I got to see most of the major cities in Europe.

One time I asked my mom what she thought I'd be and she said: "Some kind of business man". I think she was referring to the type of corporate work my father did but when I wound up as a self-employed painting contractor and apartment building owner I remembered her words and took them to heart as a type of prophecy and confirmation that all the things that I had done prior had led me to this point in life where I was exactly where I was supposed to be.

Some other words of guidance she offered from time to time: "Your father is going to hear about this when he gets home". And he did too. She was more of a loyal partner in raising her kids than she was a pal and that is what I needed most. She did all the thousands of routine things a mother does loving and raising her children and she came up short in no regard at all.

My mother a source of wisdom, example of grace and a practical guide through life.

Father

Old suit pants hung on the back of the bathroom door.

The pockets were piggy banks that fed my hungry weekends.

At the kitchen table, he'd organize his bills and do crossword puzzles.

Weeknights at dinner he'd still be wearing his starched white shirt with the collar open.

He was a rock to be avoided.

You won't get what you want and it's hard.

On Saturday's he'd become a human again and cook breakfast.

His pancakes were a fav.

On Sundays after church he'd read the whole paper and let me have the sports which I'd spread out on the living room floor and devour.

Meet the No Fun Dad.

The most fun I ever had was one night at the dinner table I injected a

bit of humor into the conversation and everyone laughed.

Giving the newest baby in the house a taste of Real Lemon was

another big laugh.!

Dad would walk us halfway to school saying things like, "c'mon,

c'mon" or "watch where you're going" when we stumbled on a crack.

We passed other kids walking by themselves on the other side of the

street as if this is the way you go through life.

Then when we reached Mitchell St. we'd have a sufficient jump start

now that the pace was set and he'd turn off to catch the train.

He put up a backboard and rim on the garage roof with the help of a

neighbor,

which was another hit. He showed me how the hot shots in his day

would shoot two handed set shots and I thought: dad they shoot

jumpers and fade aways now.

He scolded Buddha who was like forget it, the Who's Who of the neighborhood and beyond for letting loose with the F-bomb in the driveway.

In summer, there would be barbeques with hot dogs and hamburgers, potato salad and baked beans. He looked so bad in shorts and black socks, guinea T's and sandals. The less my friends saw of him the better.

They had a no-bragging-rights whatsoever used Ford Station wagon.

But the real killer was he didn't let me play football with the Rebels when all my friends were on the team but he did say I could play in high school if I still wanted to. He watched me pitch one time in high school against Seton Hall, the toughest team on the schedule and I got bombed. He sat in the car out on Central Av. past right center field. I couldn't figure him out.

When I was 15 he was being transferred to Bethlehem, Pa. and they considered moving and I was really shook. Instead he bought a VW Bug and commuted.

When I left for Vietnam he and mom were passengers as I drove the '63 Caddy I bought. He criticized me for not using a blinker when I switched lanes.

When I returned there was a "Welcome Home Charlie" banner hanging over our front porch. Our neighbor, the same neighbor who helped him install the backboard, was also a professional sign painter made it. I took it down the next day. I had my own version of coming back and fitting in swimming in my mind and it wasn't with signs and a parade.

They did let me live downstairs in the empty apartment where beer, friends and music were the norm while I worked my way back into civilian life.

Later from California he would send me mail with $10 dollars, or $20 dollars in each letter. I'd return for the holidays almost every Christmas.

One year I painted the living room and the dining room for them.

At these time's we would sit at the kitchen table together and share the whole paper. Go over the front page, politics, religion, whatever.

Then one day I got a call that he wasn't doing too well.

And then another call that I got that he was gone.

The service was done very much to my liking. The organ player sang Danny Boy and Faith of Our Fathers. My aunts and uncles seemed to be staring at me hard as the immediate family rose to exit. It was like they were searching my face for a sign of how I was doing, or for a sign of who this man was, or for traces of him in there. I straightened up even taller in my shoes if that were possible. Then as Cody's team made their way down the aisle and out of the church, two men slid

the casket in the hearse, and one with a flip of the hand shut the door

with a click and it hit me and went through me like a knife.

This show was over and dad was gone.

And I would have to carry him from here.

My Dad

taught me the basics of carpentry. I don't think we ever built

anything just the basics. Sawing wood, banging in nails. I can't even

say it was fun, just something I let him teach me... So here I am

fixing something on the house. Doing it myself. Trying to save a few

bucks. Banging in nails. Cutting the wood with the old saw. And it

all comes back to me. How he introduced me to this. Maybe that's

why I'm even doing this? How it's not that foreign to me. His

teaching me how to use the saw, how to start the cut easy and to finish the cut easy. How to hold the nail. And things are going along fine and coming out ok.

And it's sorta fun in a useful way. Beautiful day. It felt like I could say something to dad if I wanted, not really but thinking of him brought him close and he could be here with me watching and approving of everything. And so, it went like that as I was caught up in the project most of the afternoon. And how I finished up and put all the tools away and cleaned up the work site. And that we both might take a step back at this point and look at what we've done and be pleased. And I think how much is that worth to be that close to your dad again?

My mother in law and father in law are on the plane heading back

to Japan now. Probably just west of Hawaii as I write. They were

here 12 quick days, five of which were spent on a road trip. They are

the seniors in my family now and I haven't seen them in 10 years. 10

years is a long time when people " get up there". They fit right in and

just made themselves at home unpacking and using the guest

bedroom which never gets used anyway. We spent the first few days

just letting them rest and when they got rested up they did local

things and even took two trips by themselves "to explore" as they put

it. We worried the whole time they were gone. They walked down to

the Bay and back and the other time through Old Town. I went out

as a search party but they had made it safely back by the time I

returned.

Just little people, she walks slightly bent and he always dressed well,

nothing fancy. On the flight back he wore maybe a sweater and a

sport jacket, leather shoes. Simple people. Luigi our 3-yr. old pit bull

took to her and her kindly jabber right away. Him not so much, for the first two days Luigi would low growl when Dad walked into the room. But Dad was really cool and just paused and redirected his energy and I'd correct the dog. After two days they became good friends. Both would laugh repeatedly as Luigi would carry on in his playful and comical ways. Often during quiet times, you might find either one sitting in the sunroom with one of the cats in their laps.

Every night she would be helping or initiating the table setting and dishwashing and tending to the tea pot. Dad kept himself busy with his favorite computer game and I did FB. Then we'd watch the baseball games with particular interest in Boston's two Japanese relievers. He'd help her with her walker or if she got her arm stuck trying to put on a jacket he'd lend a third arm to get it straight. Watching two old people who've been together for a lifetime is a beautiful thing.

In the car on the road trip we put on a lot of miles each day and you can't help but feel uncomfortable. Sometimes they wanted to have a snack when I wanted to roll. Or my wife would remind me the window should be shut cause they get cold easily. And the radio was to be kept low so they could speak comfortably and be heard. And so, as it should be, I had to be reminded, it's not about me.

This morning we took them to the airport and stayed with them until they passed through the gate. Saying goodbye to a loved one you won't see for God knows how long, well you know how that feels. At least two or three times he thanked me for my hospitality but please, it was a gift to us. They shared my birthday cake with me last night and even sang. My wife was sitting on the back stairs. "There goes my parents' plane" she said pointing to the clouds with her face. We sat there two tender shoots planted in a quiet world. When we spoke, it was soft like the first few drops of summer rain.

Epilogue

As I walk through town with Luigi reflecting on the different phases

of my life. How when I went in the Army I handed over the power of

choice and when I returned I took it back. How it wasn't long before

I found myself tangled up in relations. My energy was spent in a

swirling storm and my potential was draining. I needed to get

somewhere where victories were easier and small things count. If

this were a story in the Bible I would compare it to Abraham taking

a knife to his son, for me it was cutting out half my heart. I was

young and believed the risk was worth it. If I didn't act now I would

never see it again the same way. By faith I saw it and by works like

Abraham I left on the proverbial journey of a thousand miles that

began with the first step.

I was using the space and the time to chase dreams. Somewhat wild

at first but paring them down as I went. Learning where my talent

lay. Learning how to put it to use. Learning that talent is what you

use to lay the foundation for good things to happen. I needed to stay

healthy and I needed a future. I needed to be building something so that one day is connected to the next with a thread of meaning running through everything. Every brick chosen had to be a trusted word or an idea I believed in. If the idea was made of inferior material I passed. I had to use quality materials that would last, put in place by workmen of good reputation. When I wasn't sure I went by word of mouth or gut feeling. I was new to this town and every friend I made and relationship I formed was a brick I added one at a time. It was all part of the house I was building in the town where I would live. It took time and focus as well as some adjustments to get all the pieces to fit and get the life I wanted.

As I walk I spot Cindy 's daughter with her daughter. Cindy had three daughters and now there are grandchildren. They're all spunky and cute but one of them was exceptionally skilled at basketball and it was a talent the other two girls didn't have. It reminds me of how much I wanted talent like that when I was in high school but in life if the talent is not yours you can want it all you want but if it's not yours there's little you can do about it but to accept it, let go and move on. That goes for much of our searching and relationships too and if you want you could call them storms and earthquakes of life because they pack the powerful emotions of disappointment and discouragement that can whip through you. Sometimes they wipe you out all at once and other times they persist and keep whipping.

We persist too and today we're in Fortuna where the river is full, swift and brown. As we walk past the Animal Rescue Center the dogs start barking longing for the life they see in me and my rescue. Luigi wouldn't trade this life for the world. Since I came along it's like he hit the lottery. His own kind will have to wait and keep barking out prayers till their own rescue angel appears. I know what it's like to feel abandoned and in need of rescue. So does Luigi and so did my dad before me. Have faith little doggies it worked out for us. Take us as proof he'll hear your cry and wipe away your tears and make up for the lost years.

The road stretches out before us like a beautiful Van Gogh painting. There was a field of yellow wildflowers beginning to pop and I thought spring cannot be far off. In the distance, the mountains were snowcapped and the bright blue sky was filled with puffy white clouds. It's true California does have everything, sun, ocean, rivers, lakes, woods, mountains, deserts and snow. When you get your life on track you give yourself a chance to have it all beautiful like that on the inside too.

And that can happen anywhere.

God bless you my friend, be persistent, resilient and strong. Have a happy life and let meaning run through it like a song. Make your mother proud. Keep bringing back days winning.

When you're young you look forward with vision.
When you're old you look back in dream like wonder
on how it all worked out.

North River

The music has ceased

stirs from the dreamland where

a sleepy voice asks what time?

and pokes around for her shoes.

I had been inhaling words in small sips for some time,

my head swims with thoughts that go nowhere.

With a large exhale a school of small fish

are released to the wild.

I always return young and unbeaten

with the first light of dawn

as fresh snow to the mountain

I am the North River

and this is my song.

The End.

Made in the USA
Middletown, DE
25 May 2020